FOREWORD

DEAR READER

There is plenty of information available about the environmental, health and moral benefits of the vegetarian diet. What I would like to bring to your attention is a metaphysical aspect.

The ancient literature of the Bhagavad Gita tells us about the inner governing principles of this universal creation. There are 3 major forces in this world that qualify everything including our thoughts, behavior, desires and all the different activities we may do in our life. These are called 'gunas' or ropes that tie us to a type of consciousness: goodness, passion and ignorance. Like colored glass through which we look at everything. Ignorance bind us with inertia, passion with greed, goodness with happiness. Among these modes goodness is the most conducive to cultivate higher values of life and assist us to practice spiritual life which in turn can liberate us from these gunas.

Food also manifests whatever consciousness the cook had at the time of cooking. Of course food in the mode of goodness has the best effect. It makes you feel relaxed and joyful. This is what the Bhagavad Gita says about it:

"Foods dear to those in the mode of goodness increase the duration of life, purify one's existence and give strength, health, happiness and satisfaction. Such foods are juicy, fatty, wholesome, and pleasing to the heart."(BG.17.8)

Therefore it is better for those who desire to practice the mode of goodness to eat food prepared by themselves or someone with a similar mind of goodness. In the Mahabharata, the great history of India it is also stated that happy are those who eat food prepared at home.

However we can take the whole experience even higher. There is a way we can make our food spiritual or transcendental to even the mode of goodness. As the sign of our maturity and growth we recognize appreciate and reciprocate with the love of our parents, other family members and dear friends in a practical way. We can also grow spiritually to start recognizing and appreciating the love of our Supreme Father and develop the desire to reciprocate with that love. To cook with love to God (Krishna) is something that He accepts with pleasure. In this way cooking becomes meditation, loving reciprocation. This deep connection to God is called 'yoga'.

In this expression of our gratitude and love our mood is that we are enthusiastic to offer the best we can, paying attention to the details.

To actually make this meditation complete we offer the prepared food to Krishna. After that we share this sanctified food with our family and friends and delight in their satisfaction. Krishna prefers food that is in the mode of goodness therefore we don't offer meat, fish, eggs, onion and garlic to Him.

In this book you find simple and inexpensive recipes with ingredients that are in the mode of goodness. Now you can add your own gratitude and love to God and after preparing you can offer it to Him. The process is simple. You can keep a corner or even just a shelf in your living room and keep it as an altar by placing pictures of God (Krishna) and spiritual teachers on it. You can decorate it as you please with nice cloths, flowers and different ornaments. You need to keep a plate, some bowls a cup and cutlery which has never been used as offering utensils and separate sponge and cloth to wash and dry them. When the meal is ready serve a portion on these utensils and place it in front of the pictures and chant 3 times:

HARE KRISHNA HARE KRISHNA
KRISHNA KRISHNAHARE HARE
HARE RAMA HARE RAMA
RAMA RAMA HARE HARE

Wait 10-15 minutes than clap your hands 3 times to announce the end of the offering than put the portion back into the rest, wash and put away whatever you used and you can enjoy your meal.

Alternatively you find the altar pictures on the back of this book. If you are sharing your accommodation with those who do not share your way of thinking you can use the book as an altar for the time of the offering, and simply put it away with the utensils after when it is completed.

I hope you will find it a fulfilling experience.

While your preparations are in the oven you can read the stories I have collected from different countries and traditions.

SOME USEFUL TIPS

   -When preparing your cake mix   butter or margarine with the sugar than mix it with the wet ingredients than add the ingredients that creates the flavor of the cake and finally mix in the flour and baking powder or baking soda if needed.

   - Temperatures are for fan ovens.

   -Vegan recipes are easily converted into veggie by replacing soya milk with milk or yoghurt and margarine with butter.

    -If you use recipes with eggs you can replace them with 2 tbsp yoghurt or soya milk or 1 per eggs.

    - Hing is a spice that gives the taste of onion to the preparation. You can buy them from big supermarkets or Asian groceries

4

Dairy Cakes

Bienenstich

You will need:
22cm spring form cake tin

Ingredients:
For the cake:
200g plain flour
25g butter
2 tbsp sugar
1 tbsp dry yeast

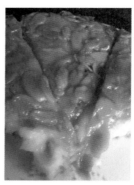

For the glaze:
30g unsalted butter
20g sugar
1tbsp honey
1tbsp double cream
30g flaked almond
1 tsp lemon juice

For the filling
250 ml double cream
25g cornflour
60g sugar
1 1/2 tsp vanilla
essence
25g butter

Method:
With the cake ingredients make a soft dough by adding warm water. Let it rise for an hour then press into the cake tin. Let it rise for another 20 min. For topping, melt butter and sugar together, when sugar dissolves add other ingredients. Spread on the top of the cake and bake for 25 min. When cool cut in half horizontally. Mix all ingredients for the filling. Constantly stirring with a whisk, bring it to the boil. Cool then spread on the bottom half of the cake and place the top half over it.

Amazing Cake

You will need:
A 25x32cm deep baking tray
and rectangular cake plate.

Ingredients:
300g caster sugar
3 tbsp yoghurt
300 ml sunflower oil
270g bananas mashed
1 tsp cinnamon
300g plain flour
1 tsp bicarbonate soda
100g pineapple chunks
drained
100g walnuts chopped

Filling and topping:
300g soft cheese
50g icing sugar
1 tsp vanilla essence

Method:
Mix all cake ingredients and pour into the
tray. Bake it for 20-25 min at 170c. Mix
ingredients for the filling. Stir well. When
cake is cooled cut it into 3 pieces. Place
one piece on a cake tray and spread some
filling on top. Repeat it with the next piece.
Then place the third piece on the top of it.
Carefully cover your cake with the rest of
the filling on the top and all four sides.
Alternatively you can use double the
amount of the Chocolate Orange cake
topping.

Berry and Lime Tart

You will need:
A deep 27x21cm baking tray

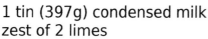

Ingredients:
1 box Ready To Use shortcrust eggfree pastry rolled
300 ml double cream
1 tin (397g) condensed milk
zest of 2 limes
4 tbsp lime juice
1 tin mixed berries
1 tbsp cornflour

Method:
Press pastry in the bottom of the tray. Bake for 15 min at 170c. Then whip the cream and mix with lime zest and condensed milk. Then gradually mix in the lime juice. Pour over the cool pastry. Put it in the fridge to set. Then drain off the juice of the berries. Put in a sauce pan and add cornflour. Bring it to the boil, then take it off the heat and add berries. Mix without breaking the fruits then spread over the top of the cake. Chill for an hour.

Black & White Cookies

You will need:
A flat baking tray with greaseproof lining

Ingredients:
250g butter softened
75g icing sugar
220g plain flour
50g cornflour
1tsp vanilla essence
2 1/2 tbsp cocoa powder
raspberry jam

Method:

Mix and knead all ingredients apart from the cocoa powder. You get a very soft dough. Put half into a piping bag with a large nozzle. Squeeze out on the baking tray in round shapes. Then knead the cocoa powder into the remaining dough and do the same again. Bake for 15-20 min at 170c. When the cookies are cool stick a white and a black one together with jam.

Caramel Cream Cake

You will need:
22cm spring form cake tin

Ingredients:
Base:
100g unsalted butter
250g ground biscuits

Filling:
175g butter
85g dark brown sugar
397g condensed milk

Topping:
fresh or tinned fruits
that go well with milk
300 ml double cream
2 tbsp icing sugar

Method:

Mix well the butter and the biscuit crumbs and press it into the bottom of the cake tin. Then chill it for 15min. Melt butter and sugar together on medium heat and add condensed milk. Bring it to the boil and let it simmer for 7-10 min. Pour over the base and let it set for 30 min. Cut the fruits into chunks and place on top of the caramel. Whip cream with the sugar and spread it on top of the fruits. Serve Chilled.

Cheesy Rolls

You will need:
flat baking tray lined with grease proof paper

Ingredients:
200g butter
200g cream cheese
1 tbsp sugar
300g plain flour
Filling:
100g ground walnuts
100g light brown sugar
1 tsp cinnamon

Method:
Make a soft dough with the first four ingredients. Separate into two halves. On a floured surface roll one half into a circle about 5-7mm thick, sprinkle it with sugar then cut it into eight. Mix ingredients for the filling and put a generous spoonful on the outer edge of each segment and roll up, placing each on the baking tray. Do the same with the other half. Bake for 20 min at 180c.

THE HAPPY MAN

Many many years ago there lived a chief in North-Africa. He was very rich and had many wives and children. But he was not happy. He thought, "I have everything. But that does not make me happy. What must I do to make me happy. I don't know"

Once he shouted angrily at his servants, "Why can't I be happy? What must I do to be happy?"

One of his servants said, "O my chief, look at the sky! How beautiful the Moon and the stars are! Look at them and you will see how good life is. That will make you happier."

"Oh, no, no, no." the chief answered angrily. "When I look at the Moon and the stars I become angry, because I know I cannot get them."

Then another servant said, "Oh my chief! What about music? Music makes a man happy. We shall play to you from morning till night and that will make you happy."

The chief's face became red with anger, "Oh, no, no, no, no!" he cried "What a silly idea. Music is fine, but to listen to music from morning till night, day after day? Never! No, never!"

So the servants went away. And the chief sat angrily in his rich room. Then one of the servants came back and made a bow, " Oh chief," he said "I think I can tell you something that will make you very happy."

"What is it?" asked the chief

"it is very easy to do," he said "you must find a happy man. Take off his shirt and put it on. Than his happiness will go into your body and you will be as happy as he is."

"I like your idea," said the chief. He send his soldiers all over the country to find a happy man. They went on and on. But it was not easy to find a happy man in the chief's country. One day the soldiers find a man in a small village who said,

"I am the happiest man in the World!" He was poor but he always smiled and sang

The soldiers brought him to the chief "At last I shall be a happy man!" said the chief and took off his shirt at once. "bring the man in!" The door of the chief's room opened. A small, dark man with a happy smile walked in.

"come here, my friend!" said the chief, "and take off your shirt!"

The happy man with a little smile came up to the chief. The chief looked him and saw. What did he see? The happy man, the happiest man in the world had no shirt!

VIKING VISDOM

Once upon a time during the Viking raids in ancient England there was a chief of the Vikings.
He was a very powerful warrior and leader but he was also a thoughtful man who above all desired wisdom.
Once he was with his advisers and generals. They were having a great feast in his hall. He turned to his chief minister and asked, "What is life and death?"
The minister was a little anxious how to answer this question so that he would be satisfied with it. As he was thinking providence provided a solution. A little bird landed on one of the hall's window ledge. Bounced around and chirped a little than flew across the hall over everybody's head and out the window at the far end.
"Did you see that?" asked the wise man.
"Yes" said the chief.
"Birth is when the bird appeared on the window ledge. Life is

when it was flying across the room and death when it left through the other window."

"Hmmm," the chief was stroking his red beard.

"Now the question is: did the bird stopped existing when it has got out of our sight?"

"No", said the chief

"Did it exist before we noticed it?"

"Yes", answered the chief.

"It is the same with life. We only see life between birth and death, but it never stops even though we are no longer perceive it."

The chief was very satisfied with this answer and rewarded his minister with gold ornaments.

HEAVEN AND HELL

Once upon a time in Japan lived a samurai. This samurai was not very strict in adhering to the principals of Bushido. He was arrogant and famous about his uncontrolled anger. He even left his master and declared himself a master. Many of his fellow samurai condemned this and said that he will go to hell.

Once on his travels he came upon a monastery. He immediately started shouting for the chief monk to come out. After some time the old monk came to the door and greeted the samurai.

-How may I serve you? - asked the monk.

-I want to know what is hell and what is heaven– said the samurai.

Without answering the old monk turned around and started to make his way back to the monastery. Immediately the samurai got very angry and pulled out his sword.

-hey! Stop! Where do you think you are going?! - he shouted with a red face.

The monk turned back and said with a peaceful smile – This is hell. Your uncontrolled anger agitates your mind. Your soul is in the prison of your hate. This is hell.

At that moment the realisation of his fallen position struck the samurai. With a humble mind he fell at the feet of the monk and begged for his mercy.

-This is heaven - said the monk – when the mind is peaceful and meek, than one is in heaven. Humility is the doorway of heaven.

Chocolate & Cola Cake

You will need:
22cm spring form
cake tin greased

Ingredients:
250g butter softened
300g sugar
75 ml milk
3 tbsp cocoa powder
250g self-raising flour
200 ml nutty cola (you can get this
 in health food shops)
1/2 tsp bicarbonate of soda

Method:

Mix all ingredients, adding cola last.
Pour mixture into the cake tin. It tends
to drip while baking so place some tin
foil under the cake tin in the oven.
Bake it for 40 min at 170c. It is nice as
it is, but it becomes irresistible If you
spread jam on the top. Whip 300 ml
double cream with 3 tbsp icing sugar
and spread it over the Jam.

Chocolate Brownie

You will need:
A deep 22x18cm
baking tray

Ingredients:
200g unsalted butter
200g dark chocolate
1/2 cup double cream
270g caster sugar
40g cocoa powder
100g plain flour
50g white chocolate
50g milk chocolate

Method:
Break dark chocolate into pieces, put in a
bowl with the butter. Place on the top of
boiling water to melt gently stiring all the
while. Whisk double cream until firm. Add
sugar and whisk it a bit more. Pour chocolate
mixture into the cream and gently mix
together. Add flour and chop white and milk
chocolate into small pieces and mix all
together. Bake for 30 min at 170c. Serve
chilled.

Date slice

You will need:
A deep 27x21cm
baking tray

Ingredients:

375g muscovado sugar
375g self-raising flour
185g butter
375g chopped dates
3 tbsp oats
1/2 tsp cinnamon
3 tbsp yoghurt

Method:

Pour 9 tbsp boiling water over the dates
leave for 5 minutes, then blend to a paste
in a food processor.
Put sugar, flour, butter into a bowl and rub
together until crumb like. Tip half the
mixture into another bowl and stir in the
yoghurt and cinnamon. You will get a
moist dough. Press this evenly into the
base of the tray. Spread the date paste
over the dough. Mix oats into the other
mixture and sprinkle over the date paste
pressing down lightly. Bake for 25 min at
170c.

RITUAL CAT

In a Zen monastery the monks gathered every evening for meditation. When the spiritual teacher and his disciples began their evening meditation, a cat who lived in the monastery made such noise that it distracted them. It went on for some time. One day the teacher ordered that the cat be tied up during the evening practice.

Years later, when the teacher died, the cat continued to be tied up during the meditation session. And when the cat eventually died, another cat was brought to the monastery and tied up.

Centuries later, learned descendants of the spiritual teacher wrote scholarly treatises about the religious significance of tying up a cat for meditation practice.

THE ROBE

Wealthy patrons invited Ikkyu a zen master to a banquet. Ikkyu arrived dressed in his beggar's robes.

The host, not recognising him, chased him away. Ikkyu went home, changed into his ceremonial robe of purple brocade, and returned.

With great respect, he was received into the banquet room. There, he put his robe on the cushion, saying, "I expect you invited the robe since you showed me away a little while ago," and left.

THE PROUD KING

Long time ago in India there lived a king named Janashruti. He was a very pious king. He opened hospitals universities and looked after the citizens welfare in every way. He was very satisfied with himself thinking that he was very pious. This had made him proud.

Two sages had noticed this and they was worried for the king, because pride is a quality that can be the downfall of a pious person. So they devised a plan to save the king. They took the shapes of swans and was flying over the the royal palace. The king was resting on the roof. As they were flying one of the swans sad: "Oh look there is Maharaj Janashruti. He is such a pious king. Make sure you don't fly over him." The other swan replied:" I know he thinks that he will get all the credits for his piety and he will be in heaven as the result. But he does not know that all his credit will go to a saintly person called Dhaumya who is living in poverty in his city. He has transcendental knowledge therefore he attract all the pious credits"

Hearing this King Janashruti felt greatly disturbed. He was doing all this good and someone else gets the credit! Immediately called his ministers and ordered them to find the saint, and do not come back until they find him.

The ministers after days of searching find a ascetic man lying under a cart and stretching his body. They reported it to the King. "why didn't you bring him here?" asked the king loosing his patience.

" he would not come into such an opulent residence. You better go to him." said the minister.

So the king took some money and went to see the holy man.

" Please take this money and teach me transcendental knowledge otherwise I will loose all my pious credits!" asked the man.

"Away with you low class person! I do not want your money and you do not deserve transcendental knowledge." shouted the man.

The king humiliated went back to the palace. Gathered all his wealth and his daughter and went back to the holy man. "Please take my wealth and my daughter" He fell at the feet of the saint with great respect.

"I can see that you are ready to sacrifice everything, therefore I am willing to teach you and you can keep your wealth and give your daughter to a prince." answered the man.

"First please tell me why did you called me law class earlier?" asked the king humbly.

"Because you were lamenting. Only law class people lament. A king do not. And knowledge should not be given to a low class person because they will use it for their selfish ends. My harsh words has purified your heart and you are now free from pride. Hence you are a suitable candidate for transcendental knowledge"

Drum Cake

You will need:
22cm spring form
cake tin base

Ingredients:
For the cake:
500g plain flour
300g butter
200g sugar
100 ml milk
For the top:
200g sugar
1 tsp butter
1 tbsp lemon juice

For the cream:
600g double cream
250g icing sugar
3 tbsp cocoa powder
200g chocolate
250g butter
1 tsp vanilla essence

Method:
Knead cake ingredients together. Divide into
six. Roll the first one into a round shape,
same size as the tin base. Bake it on the tin
base for 15 min. Repeat with the other 5. Put
the top ingredients into a saucepan and boil
until it becomes runny and brown. Spread it
on one of the pastries. While it is still hot with
an oiled knife cut it into 12 slices. For the
filling whip double cream with icing sugar,
vanilla and cocoa. Melt chocolate and butter
and mix with cream. Cover all the layers and
the side of the cake. Place the sugar covered
pastry on the top.

Honey Lamingtons

You will need:
A deep 27x21cm
baking tray

Ingredients:
150 ml milk
2 tbsp yoghurt
50g butter melted
300g sugar
5 tbsp honey melted
375g self-raising
flour

For the covering:
220g butter
250g sugar
50g cocoa powder
2 tbsp orange juice
200g dessicated coconut

Method:

Mix all ingredients. Bake for about 35-40 min.
While cooling melt the topping ingredients
over medium heat. Pour coconut into a tray.
Cut the cake into smallish pieces (about
4x4cm). When the chocolate cream is cool
enough to touch drop one of the pieces in it.
Cover the piece in chocolate on all sides then
roll in the coconut and place on a tray. Do all
of them like this. This cake is best served
after a day or two.

Honey Lamingtons

You will need:
A deep 27x21cm
baking tray

Ingredients:
150 ml milk
2 tbsp yoghurt
50g butter melted
300g sugar
5 tbsp honey melted
375g self-raising
flour

For the covering:
220g butter
250g sugar
50g cocoa powder
2 tbsp orange juice
200g dessicated coconut

Method:

Mix all ingredients. Bake for about 35-40 min.
While cooling melt the topping ingredients
over medium heat. Pour coconut into a tray.
Cut the cake into smallish pieces (about
4x4cm). When the chocolate cream is cool
enough to touch drop one of the pieces in it.
Cover the piece in chocolate on all sides then
roll in the coconut and place on a tray. Do all
of them like this. This cake is best served
after a day or two.

THE STARFISH STORY

One day somewhere in America, a man was walking along the beach early in the morning. He notice a boy in the distance. He looked like he was dancing. The man found this interesting, so he went closer to see what the boy was actually doing.

When he was close enough he realized that the boy was picking something up and gently throwing it into the ocean.

Approaching the boy, he asked, "What are you doing?"

The youth replied,"Throwing starfish back into the ocean. The surf is up and the tide is going out. If I don't throw them back they will die."

"son," the man said, "don't you realize there are miles and miles of beach and hundreds and thousands of starfish? You cannot make a difference! It's a waste of time!"

After listening politely the boy bent down, picked up another starfish and threw it back into the surf. Then, smiling at the man he said, "I made a difference to that one.

THE MAGIC RING (Sufi)

A powerful king, ruler of many domains, was in a position of such magnificence that wise men were his mere employees. And yet one day he felt himself confused and called the sages to him. He said:

'I do not know the cause, but something impels me to seek a certain ring, one that will enable me to stabilize my state. 'I must have such a ring. And this ring must be one which, when I am unhappy, will make me joyful. At the same time, if I am happy and look upon it, I must be made sad.'

The wise men consulted one another, and threw themselves into deep contemplation, and finally they came to a decision as to the character of this ring which would suit their king. The ring which they devised was one upon which was inscribed the legend:

This, too will pass

THE BOY AND THE DRUM

There was once a small boy who banged a drum all day and loved every moment of it. He would not be quiet, no matter what anyone else said or did. Various people who called themselves Sufis, and other well-wishers, were called in by neighbors and asked to do something about the child.
The first so-called Sufi told the boy that he would, if he continued to make so much noise, perforate his eardrums; this reasoning was too advanced for the child, who was neither a scientist nor a scholar. The second told him that drum beating was a sacred activity and should be carried out only on special occasions. The third offered the neighbors plugs for their ears; the fourth gave the boy a book; the fifth gave the neighbors books that described a method of controlling anger through biofeedback; the sixth gave the boy meditation exercises to make him placid and explained that all reality was imagination. Like all placebos, each of these remedies worked for a short while, but none worked for very long.
Eventually, a real Sufi came along. He looked at the situation, handed the boy a hammer and chisel, and said, "I wonder what is INSIDE the drum?"

Almond Tarts

You will need:
A 12 hole tartlet tin

Ingredients:
375g pack ready to roll
shortcrust pastry
75g unsalted butter
110g curd cheese
3 tbsp double cream
75g caster sugar
50g ground almonds
zest of 1 lemon

Method:

Cut out 12 circles of pastry, each 10cm wide
and line each hole in the tin. In a bowl mix
all ingredients until they are smooth. Spoon
the mixture into the pastry cases and bake
for 20-25 min. This delicious tart reportedly
was made for King Henry VIII by Anne
Boleyn when she was the Maid of Honor of
Catherine of Aragon.

New York Cheesecake

You will need:
22cm spring form cake tin

Ingredients:

140g plain flour
1/4 tsp baking powder
50g caster sugar
50g unsalted butter
little water
600g cream cheese
150g caster sugar
1 tsp vanilla essence
300 ml double cream

Method:

Making the base: Knead together the first 5 ingredients, then press it into the bottom of the cake tin. Bake for 10 min. Optionally you can spread jam or date paste over it when it is cool.
 Making the topping: Beat together cream cheese, sugar and vanilla essence. Whip the cream and mix it all together spread it on the top of the base and bake it at 170c until golden brown. It takes about and hour. In the picture I have put whipped cream and blueberries on the top.

Nutty Brownie

You will need:
A deep 27x21cm
baking tray

Ingredients:

For the base:
225g plain flour
80g light
muscovado sugar
100g melted butter
50g melted plain
chocolate

For the top:
120g dark muscovado
sugar
70g butter
40g golden syrup
1 tbsp double cream
300g mixed nuts
toasted

Method:

Mix together the base ingredients and press
evenly into the baking tray. Bake for 15 min.
Meanwhile make the topping. Put sugar,
butter and golden syrup into a pan over
medium heat. stirring often to dissolve the
sugar, but don't bring to boil. Add cream
then the nuts. Spread over the base and
bake it for another 10 min and let it cool.

Oat Cookies

You will need:
A flat baking tray lined with baking paper

Ingredients:
110g salted butter
220g light brown sugar
110g self-raising flour
110g nuts, dried fruits or chock chips to your taste
2 tbsp yoghurt
2 tbsp water
1 tsp vanilla essence
250g oats

Method:

Put all ingredients into a large bowl and mix well. Roll them into table tennis ball sizes and place them onto the baking tray slightly flattening them.
Bake for 15-20 min at 180c. When ready cool them on a wire rack. You can spread melting chococlate or lemon icing on the top.
For vegan alternative use margarine instead of butter, and soya milk instead of the yoghurt and a handful more flour.

Orange &White Chocolate Cake

You will need:
2x22cm spring form cake tin

Ingredients:
175g butter softened
175g caster sugar
Zest of 4 oranges, juice of 1
1/2 cup of yoghurt
100g self-raising flour
1 tsp baking powder
100g ground almonds

For the icing:
200g white chocolate
200ml creme fraiche

Method:
Gradually mix all the ingredients for the cake. Divide the mix between the tins and bake for 30-35 min. To make the icing melt white chocolate. Whip creme fraiche until thick, then fold in the white chocolate mix gently. When the cakes are cool place one of them on a serving plate, spread half of the topping on it then place the other cake on the top and spread the remaining topping over it.

THE STORY OF THE ROSES

In the latter half of 1838, Cherokee People who had not voluntarily moved West earlier, were forced to leave their home in the east

The trail to the west was long and treacherous and many were dying along the way. The People's heart were heavy with sadness and their tears mingled with the dust of the trail. The elders knew that the survival of the children depended upon the strength of the women.

One evening around the camp fire, the elders called upon Heaven Dweller ga-lv-la-di-he-hi. They told Him of the People's suffering and tears. They were afraid the children will not survive to rebuild the Cherokee Nation.

Ga-lv-la-di-he-hi spoke to them, "To let you know how much I care, I will give you a sign. In the morning tell the women to look back along the trail. Where their tears have fallen, I will cause to grow a plant that will have seven leaves for the seven clans of the Cherokee. Amidst that plant will be a delicate white rose with five petals. In the centre of that blossom will be a pile of gold to remind the Cherokeeof the white man's greed for the gold found in the Cherokee homeland. This plant will be sturdy and strong with thorns on all the stems. It will defy anything which tries to destroy it."

The next morning the elders told the women to look back down the trail. A plant was growing fast and covering the trail where they have walked. As the women watched, blossoms formed and slowly opened. They forgot their sadness. Like the plant protected it's blossoms, they knew they would have the courage and determination to protect their children who would begin a new Nation in the West.

THE LOST SON (China)

A young widower, who loved his five year old son very much was away on busyness when bandits came and burned down the whole village, taking his son away. When the man returned, he saw the ruins and panicked. He took the burned corpse of an infant to be his son and cried uncontrollably. He organized a cremation ceremony, collected the ashes and put them in a beautiful little bag which he always kept with him.

Soon afterward, his real son escaped from the bandits and found his way home. He arrived at his father's new cottage at midnight and knocked on the door.

The father still grieving asked, "Who is it?"

The child answered, "It's me, Papa, open the door!"

But in his agitated state of mind, convinced that his son was dead, the father thought that some young boy was making fun of him. He shouted, "Go away" and continued to cry.

After some time the child left.

Father and son never saw each other again.

After this story the Buddha said: "Sometime, somewhere you take something to be the truth. If you cling to it so much, even when the truth comes in person and knocks on your door, you will not open it."

HOW DOES READING THE BHAGAVAD-GITA HELP?

An old farmer lived in the mountains with his grandson. Each morning the Grandpa was up early, and reading his Bhagavad-Gita. His grandson wanted to be just like him and tried to imitate him in every way he could.

One day the grandson asked, "Grandpa! I try to read the Bhagavad-Gita just like you, but I don't understand it, and what I do understand I forget as soon as I close the book. What good does reading the Bhagavad-Gita do?"

The grandfather quietly turned from putting coal in the stove and replied, "Take this coal basket down to the river and bring me back a basket of water."

The boy did as he was told, but all the water leaked out before he got back to the house. The grandfather laughed and said, "You will have to move a little faster next time." and send him back to the river to try again.

This time the boy ran faster, but again the basket was empty before he returned home. Out of breath he told his grandfather that it is impossible to carry water in a basket, and he went to get a bucket instead. The old man said, "I don't want a bucket of water I want a basket of water. You are just not trying hard enough, " he went out the door to watch the boy try again.

At this point the boy knew it was impossible, but he wanted to show his grandfather that even if he ran as fast as he could the water would leak out before he got back to the house. When he got back, out of breath he said, "Look! It is useless!"

"So, you think it is useless?" The old man said, "Look at the basket.

The boy looked the basket and realized that the basket was transformed from a dirty coal basket to clean one inside and out.

"Son that is what happens when you read Bhagavad-Gita. You might not understand or remember everything, but when you read it, you will be changed, inside and out. That is the work of Krishna in our lives."

THE STORY OF PRINCE DHRUVA (India)

In the dawn of mankind there lived a king who had two queens. Both queens had a son, but the king favoured the younger queen over the older one. The older queen, Suniti's son was named Dhruva.

Once upon a time, the king was patting the son of his favourite queen, placing him on his lap. The five years old Dhruva was also trying to get on the king's lap, but the king did not very much welcome him. Noticing it, his step mother began to speak with envy:"My dear child, you do not deserve to sit on the throne or on the lap of the king. Surely you are also the son of the king, but because you did not take your birth from my womb, you are not qualified to sit on your father's lap."Prince Dhruva having been struck by the strong words of his stepmother, became overwhelmed with anger and went to his mother. When she heard the story, Suniti also became greatly aggrieved. Not finding any remedy she said to her son: "Anyone who inflicts pains upon others suffers himself from that pain. Whatever my co-wife said is so, because the king feels ashamed of me. Therefore you have taken birth from an unfortunate woman. Therefore I cannot help you. Only God can help you, who is so great that He is worshiped even by the greatest of men. I cannot see anyone else that can give you shelter. I know that the sages go to the forest and practice asceticism to meet this Supreme Deity."Hearing this, prince Dhruva immediately set out to the forest. He began severe austerities, so much so that he drew the attention of the great saint Narada who came to speak with him, "Dear boy, you are only a child whose attachment is sports and other frivolities.

Why are you so affected by words insulting your honor? These austerities of yours will not be successful. It is better that you go home."Prince Dhruva was unmoved by Narada's words and was determined to stay in the forest until he met God and asked Him for a kingdom greater than that of his father's.

Many years passed. He was performing his austerities and meditation with great self-control. Finally one day, Dhruva's meditation suddenly broke. He opened his eyes and beheld in front of him the Lord of all the Universes. Dhruva became overwhelmed with devotion, becoming peaceful and completely happy, forgetting his anger.

The Lord asked Dhruva if he desired anything from Him.

Prince Dhruva said: "I was looking for broken glass, but I find a priceless gem. I do not have any wish other than to remember you all the time."

The Lord was pleased with prince Dhruva and blessed him by giving him a planet to rule over. This planet is the pole star.

PRUNES FOR DIRT (Bulgaria)

Somewhere in Bulgaria there lived a well-to-do man who had a son.

When his son became a young man, he was thinking that it is time for him to get married. He thought about how to find a good wife for his son. Then he had an idea.

He had a lot of prunes. He packed them in bags and put them on his cart. Then he sat his son next to him on the cart and started to go around the town, shouting, "Prunes for dirt! Prunes for rubbish!"

The ladies of the town quickly gathered dirt and rubbish from their houses into bags and came out to give it to the man. For one bag of rubbish he gave a bag of prunes. The girls came with big bags of dirt.

Finally a young and shy girl came with a handful of dirt: "Sir, I only have this much dirt in our house, I don't know if it is enough to get some of your prunes?"

"Dear girl," answered the man, "for this much dirt I can give you my son, if you are willing to accept my proposal!"

ALEXANDER AND DIOGENES

It was in Corinth that a meeting between Alexander the Great and Diogenes is supposed to have taken place.

Once, Diogenes was relaxing in the sunlight in the morning in front of his clay wine jar he was living in. Alexander, thrilled to meet the famous philosopher, asked if there was any favor he might do for him.

Diogenes replied, "Yes, don't take away what you cannot give. Stand out of my sunlight."

Alexander then declared, "If I were not Alexander, then I should wish to be Diogenes."

Pineapple Cake

You will need:
A deep 22x18 cm baking tray

Ingredients:

For the topping:
100g butter
100g light muscovado sugar
520g canned pineapple chunks drained
Glace cherries

For the cake:
75g dessicated coconut
150g butter softened
300g caster sugar
1/2 cup yoghurt
3 tsp vanilla extract
260g plain flour
1 1/2 tsp baking powder

Method:

Start with the topping. Melt the butter and sugar in a saucepan over medium heat for a few minutes. Place the pineapple chunks in the bottom of the baking tray and fill up the gap between them with cherries. Pour over the butter. For the cake roast the coconut until it becomes light brown. Grind it fine in a blender. Add the next four ingredients and blend until smooth. Pour it into a bowl and mix in the flour and baking powder. Spoon it into the baking tray over the pineapples and bake it for 35-40 min When cool turn it out onto a flat tray upside down.

Sandwich Bisquits

You will need:
A large flat
baking tray

Ingredients:
170g ground nuts
170g plain flour
170g butter
115g caster sugar
rind of 1 lemon
1 tsp vanilla essence
Jam

Method:

Knead all the igredients together. Roll out
5-7mm thick cut it with a pastry cutter.
Place them on the baking tray and bake
for 15 min. When cooled Put half a jar of
jam into a pan add a bit of lemon juice
and bring it to a boil. Spread it on half of
the bisquits and place another one on the
top of them. They are very nice like this
but you can top them with melting
chocolate to make them even more
appealing.

Strawberry Cheesecake Brownie

You will need:
22cm spring form
cake tin greased

Ingredients:
Brownie:
200g choc chips
200g unsalted butter
200g icing sugar
150g plain flour
Cream cheese:
400g cream cheese
150g icing sugar
1 tsp vanilla essence
150ml double cream

Topping:
300ml double cream
50g icing sugar
1 tsp pink food colouring
1 tsp strawberry
essence

Method:
Mix brownie ingredients, bake it for 10 min at 170c. You can put tin foil under the cake tin in case the butter starts dripping. Beat cream cheese, sugar, vanilla together and mix in cream. Whisk until thick, then spread on the top of the cooled brownie. Whisk together topping ingredients and spread on the cake. Serve chilled.

Toffee pudding

You will need:
A deep 27x21cm
baking tray

Ingredients:
200g dates
50g soft butter
175g demerara sugar
1 tbsp golden syrup
2 tbsp black treacle
4 tbsp yoghurt
1 tsp vanilla essence
200g self-raising flour
1 tsp bicarbonate of soda
For the sauce:
100g brown sugar
100g butter
200 ml double cream

Method:
Cook dates in a little water until soft. Put in
blender add next 6 ingredients and blend until
smooth. Add flour and bicarbonate of soda,
mix well. Pour into tray and bake for 35 min at
170c. Melt butter and sugar together add
cream and boil for a few min. Pour sauce on
top of the slices when serving.

THE FOOLISH BRAHMIN (India)

Once upon a time, a foolish brahmin came to visit Birbal with a strange request. He wanted to be addressed as "pandit".

Now, the term "pandit" refers to a man of learning. But unfortunately this poor brahmin was uneducated. Birbal tried to explain the difference to him, saying that it was not correct to call an uneducated man a pandit, and because of this very reason it would be improper to call him so.

But the silly brahmin had his heart set on this title.

So, as usual, Birbal had a brilliant idea. He said that as the brahmin was an uneducated man, he should hurl abuses and stones at anyone who dared to address him by the very same title he wanted. Then Birbal called all his servants to himself and ordered them to call this lowly brahmin a pandit. The brahmin was very pleased. But the moment the servants started calling out to him as "pandit", he pretended to be very angry and started to abuse them loudly. Then he picked up a few stones and hurled them in their direction. All as per the clever Birbal's advice.

All this shouting and screaming drew a crowd. When people realized that this brahmin was erupting every time anyone called him "pandit", they all started to tease him. Over the next couple of days he would constantly hear the refrain "pandit" wherever he went. Very soon the whole town started referring to him as "pandit", much to his delight.

The foolish brahmin never realised why people were calling him in this manner, and was extremely pleased with the result. He thanked Birbal from the very bottom of his foolish heart.

KRISHNA'S MERCY (India)

Emperor Akbar (1542 –1605) of India, was known as a person who had appreciation for the diversity of religions in his kingdom. His prime minister named Birbal was a wise Hindu.

One day the emperor cut his finger. Birbal, instead of showing the same sympathy as the other ministers, gravely said: "It is Lord Krishna's mercy."

The emperor was furious: "If I put you into prison, will that also be "Lord Krishna's mercy"?!"

"Oh yes, indeed," answered Birbal.

The emperor with great anger asked for the guards to take Birbal and put him into jail.

Next day Akbar went out to hunt. Somehow in the forest he lost his companions and the way back to the palace. As he was wandering alone, he came by some dacoits who wanted a human for their sacrifice for the pleasure of Durga. Just as they were about to kill him, one of them noticed the cut on the emperor's finger. After some discussion they decided that he was unfit for their purpose, and set him free.

Back at the palace, Akbar was very sorry about his anger at his wise minister and called for him. After apologizing the emperor asked, "I understand that the cut on my finger was your Lord Krishna's mercy, but what about your being in prison?"

"If you didn't imprison me I would have been with you in the forest, and because I didn't have any wounds the dacoits would have surely sacrificed me. So yes, it was also Lord Krishna's mercy."

Vegan Cakes

Apple Cake

You will need:

A deep 27x21cm
baking tray

Ingredients:

250g margarine
1/2 cup soya milk
250g light muscovado sugar
150g chopped dates
150g chopped hazelnuts
500g self-raising flour
3 tsp cinnamon
3 medium eating apples
1/4 jar peach jam

Method:

Melt margarine and mix with soya milk and
sugar. Peel and dice two of the apples add to
the mix along with the rest of the ingredients.
Fold mixture into the prepared tray and smooth
the top. Thinly slice the last apple (unpeeled)
cut out the core and place the slices neatly on
the top of the cake mixture. Bake for 50 min at
170c. When ready heat up jam with a little
water, boil for a few seconds and pour over on
the top of the cake.

THE GREEDY MAN

Once upon a time there lived a man who was always hankering for more riches. He was very careful not to spend a penny, if it was absolutely unavoidable. He was just saving and saving.

When he grew old, he was considering his future after his death. Something within him was afraid that the way he was saving all his money was not completely righteous. So he thought about how to make it right.

Finally he found the solution: He went to the church and donated ten pounds to the priest. He felt satisfied.

On the day he died, he met God.

God said to him, "In all your life you have acted selfishly, thinking only of yourself. Therefore you will have to go to hell."

The man protested, "I have given ten pounds to the priest in the church! Surely I am a good man and do not deserve to suffer in hell!"

God thought about it for a moment and said: "I give your money back and you go to hell."

Apple & Cinnamon Cake

You will need:

A deep 27x21cm
baking tray

Ingredients:

180ml sunflower oil
6 tbsp soya milk
180ml apple juice
150g light muscovado sugar
250g sultanas
1 1/2 tsp cinnamon
4 apples (not peeled) grated
375g self-raising flour
1 1/2 tsp baking powder

Method

It is a very simple cake. Just mix all
ingredients in the same order as listed
above. Fold mixture into baking tray and
bake for 40 min. When cool sprinkle with
icing sugar.

Blueberry Cake

You will need:
22cm spring form cake tin

Ingredients:
250g blueberries
225g margarine
225g caster sugar
9 tbsp soya milk
1 tsp vanilla essence
150g self-raising
 flour
75g ground almonds

Topping:
100g margarine
200g icing sugar
1 1/2 tsp vanilla
essence

Method:
Use baking parchment in the bottom of your tin. Wash and dry blueberries and spread them in the tin.

Mix well margarine, sugar, soya milk and vanilla essence. Then add almonds and flour mix well until smooth. Spread on the top of the blueberries. Bake for 35-40 min at 170c. The margarine may start dripping when melted so it is safer to put aluminium foil under your tin. When ready let it cool and turn it upside down on a tray. Pull off the baking paper. Mix remaining ingredient until smooth and spread on the top of the cake.

LORD CAITANYA AND THE LEPER

Lord Caitanya (1486–1534), born in west Bengal, was a Vaishnava saint and social reformer in eastern India, worshiped by followers of Gaudiya Vaishnavism as the full incarnation of Lord Krishna.

On His tours in south India He visited all the holy places, met numerous devotees and spread the chanting of the holy names of Krishna.

Once while traveling, he entered a village where he spent a night at a brahmana's house. He accepted his hospitality and exchanged kind words with his family, teaching them about devotion to Lord Krishna. Next morning he left, to continue on His way.

In the area lived a brahmana named Vasudeva, who suffered from leprosy. Although suffering, the brahmana Vasudeva was enlightened.

Then one night, Vasudeva heard of Lord Caitanya's arrival, and in the morning he came to see the Lord at the house where He stayed. When he arrived he was informed that the Lord already left. The leper then fell unconscious in lamentation.

Lord Caitanya understood the pain of Vasudeva in his heart, and turned back. When He saw Vasudeva, he immediately embraced him. As soon as He touched him, both the leprosy and his distress went away. Indeed, Vasudeva's body became very beautiful. Ecstatic, he began to speak:

"O my merciful Lord, such mercy is not possible for an ordinary man. Such mercy can be found only in you. Upon seeing me, even a sinful person goes away due to my bad bodily odor. Yet You have touched me, such is the independent behavior of the Supreme Personality of Godhead."

Being meek and humble, the brahmana Vasudeva worried that he would become proud after being cured by the grace of the Lord.

Lord Caitanya advised him to chant the Hare Krishna mantra incessantly. By doing so he would never become unnecessarily proud.

Such is the power of chanting: "Hare Krishna, Hare Krishna, Krishna Krishna, Hare Hare, Hare Rama, Hare Rama, Rama Rama, Hare Hare".

TO HEAR THE UNHEARD

Back in the third century A.D., The King Ts'ao sent his son, Prince T'ai, to a temple to study under the great master Pan Ku. Because the Prince T'ai was to succeed his father as king, Pan Ku was to teach the boy the basics of being a good ruler. When the prince arrived at the temple, the master sent him alone to the Ming-Li Forest. After one year, the prince was to return to the temple to describe the sound of the forest.
When Prince T'ai returned, Pan Ku asked the boy to describe all that he could hear.

"Master," replied the prince, "I could hear the cuckoos sing, the leaves rustle, the hummingbirds hum, the crickets chirp, the grass blow, the bees buzz, and the wind whisper and holler." When the prince had finished, the master told him to go back to the forest to listen to what more he could hear. The prince was puzzled by the master's request, had he not discerned every sound already?
For days and nights on end, the young prince sat alone in the forest listening, but he heard no sounds other than those he had already heard. Then one morning, as the prince sat silently beneath the trees, he started to discern faint sounds unlike those he had ever heard before.

The more acutely he listened, the clearer the sounds became. A feeling of enlightenment enveloped the boy. "These must be the sounds the master wished me to discern," he reflected.

When Prince T'ai returned to the temple, the master asked him what more he had heard.

"Master," responded the prince reverently, "when I listened most closely, I could hear the unheard - the sound of flowers opening, the sound of the sun warming the earth, and the sound of the grass drinking the morning dew..."

The master nodded approvingly. "To hear the unheard," remarked Pan Ku, "is a necessary discipline to be a good ruler, for only when a ruler has learned to listen closely to the people's hearts, hearing their feelings un-communicated, pains unexpressed, and complaints not spoken of, can he hope to inspire confidence in his people, understand when something is wrong, and meet the true needs of his citizens.

The demise of states comes when leaders listen only to superficial words and do not penetrate deeply into the souls of their people to hear their true opinions, feelings and desires."

Capuccino Cake

You will need:
A deep 27x21cm
baking tray

Ingredients:
1 tsp cocoa powder
2 tbspinstant coffee
granules
225g margarine
225g caster sugar
1/2 cup soya milk
225g self-raising flour
1 tsp baking powder

Topping:
3/4 cup soya milk
3/4 cup icing sugar
1 cup sunflower oil
1 1/2 tsp vanilla
  essence
lemon juice

Method:
Mix cocoa and coffee granules with 2 tbsp
warm water. Put all cake ingredients into
a large bowl and beat with an electric
hand whisk for 2 min. Tip the mixture into
the tray, level out and bake it for 35 min
on 170c. Put soya milk, icing sugar,
vanilla essence and oil into a blender.
Blend for 10 sec than gradually add
lemon juice to it while blending until the
mixture thickens. When the cake is
cooled spread the topping mixture on top,
dust it with cocoa powder.

Carrot Cake

You will need:
A deep 27x21cm
baking tray

Ingredients:

250g light muscovado
sugar
250ml sunflower oil
1/2 cup soya milk
200g carrot finely grated
150g raisins
zest of two oranges
1 1/2 tsp cinnamon
3/4 tsp nutmeg
250g self-raising flour
1/2 tsp bicarbonate of soda

Method:

Mix all ingredients and bake for 40 min at
170c. When cool make frosting mixing 2
tbsp orange juice and as much icing sugar
as it takes to become quite thick like
double cream. Drizzle it on the top of the
cooled cake.

Chocolate and Orange Cake

You will need:
22cm spring form cake tin

Ingredients:
1 orange
100g chocolate broken into pieces
6 tbsp soya milk
280g caster sugar
240g margarine
25g cocoa powder
250g plain flour
1 1/2 tsp baking powder

For the topping:
250g caster sugar
1tbsp golden syrup
60g cocoa powder
300 ml water
100g cornflour
40g margarine
1/2 tsp vanilla essence

Method:
Pierce the orange with a skewer. Cook it until soft (30 min). Then blend in a food processor until smooth. Melt the chocolate, then mix all the cake ingredients together. Bake it for 50-60 min. For the topping melt together on medium heat the sugar, cocoa powder and golden syrup with 200ml of the water. Mix cornflour with the remaining water and bring it to the boil. add remaining ingredients. Chill before spreading on top of the cake.

Chocolate Cake

You will need:
2x22cm spring
form cake tin

Ingredients:
1 3/4 cup hot water with
4 tbsp instant coffee
2/3 cup cocoa powder
1 1/2 cup sugar
1/3 cup sunflower oil
1/3 cup apple juice
1/4 cup cornflour
2 cups plain flour
1 tsp bicarbonate of soda
1 1/2 tsp baking powder
For topping
200g margarine
400g icing sugar
6 tbsp cocoa powder
2 tsp vanilla essence

Method:
Mix all ingredients and share it between
the tins. Bake it for about 45 min. When
cool mix topping ingredients with a
spoon and spread on the top of the
cakes than place them on the top of
each other. Exellent birthday cake.

JESUS AND THE DYING MAN

When Lord Jesus was traveling around Judea, some women came crying and begging for his help: "Please Rabbi, come to our house our husband is dying!"

Jesus went to see the man. He was only a skeleton with no flesh on his bones. He was so weak that he could hardly speak. A huge crowd gathered to see Jesus doing a miracle. Yet Jesus only said that he wanted the man to fast for forty days.

People were shocked: "To fast?! He will not survive!" Half of the crowd left in disappointment.

After forty days Jesus came back. Some people who still had faith in him gathered. Jesus then instructed the man's wife to heat up some milk with honey. He held the cup of steaming milk to the man's mouth but said to him not to drink.

Some people become angry: "He is torturing him on his death bed!" and they left.

After some time however the worms from the belly of the man started to come out, lured by the smell of the milk, since they had been starving for forty days. This was the cause of the man's illness.

Than Jesus let the man drink the milk and said: "Your faith has saved you.

KRISHNA HAS JUSTICE AND PLAN FOR EVERYONE

Once there was a sweeper in a well-known Krishna temple and he was very sincere and devoted. Every time he saw thousands of devotees coming to take see the Lord, he thought that the Lord is standing all the time He must be feeling very tired.

So one day, he asked the Lord whether he could take the place of the Lord for a day, so that the Lord could have some rest.

The Deity of Krishna replied, "I do not mind taking a break. I will transform you to be like Myself, but you must do one thing. You must just stand here like Me, smile at everyone and just give benedictions. Do not interfere with anything and do not say anything. Just have faith that I have a master plan for everything."

The sweeper agreed to this.

The next day the sweeper took the position of the Deity and stood up on the altar. First a rich man came and prayed to the Lord. He offered some donation and prayed that his business would prosper. While going, the rich man inadvertently left his wallet full of money right there.

Now the sweeper, in the form of the Deity could not call him and so he decided to control himself and keep quiet.

Next a poor man came and he put one coin in the donation box, and prayed to the Lord that he could continue to be engaged in the Lord's service. He also said that his family was in dire need of some basic things. But he left it in the good hands of the Lord to give some solution.

When he opened his eyes, he saw the wallet left by the rich man. The poor man thinking that the Lord very kindly answered his prayer thanked the Lord for His kindness and took the wallet very innocently.

The sweeper, in the form of the Deity could not say anything, and he had to just keep on smiling.

At that point a sailor walked in. He prayed for his safe journey, as he was going on a long trip. Just then, the rich man came back with the police, and seeing the sailor there he asked the police to arrest him, thinking that he has taken his wallet. The policeman grabbed the sailor who was shocked and disturbed.

The sailor looked at the Lord in despair and asked why he, an innocent person, was being punished.

The sweeper, in the form of the Deity could take no more, and he started speaking. He said that the sailor was not the thief, but it was the poor man who took away the wallet. The rich man was very thankful, as was the sailor.

At night, the Lord came and He asked the sweeper how his day had been.

The sweeper said, "I thought it would have been easy, but now I know that Your days are not so easy... But I did one good thing." Then he explained the whole episode to the Lord.

The Lord became very grave. He asked, "Why did you not just stick to our plan? You had no faith in Me. Do you think that I do not understand the hearts of all those who come here?

All the donations which the rich man gave were stolen money, and they are only a fraction of what he really has, whereas he wants Me to reciprocate unlimitedly.

The single coin offered by the poor man was the last coin he had, and he gave it to Me out of love.

If the sailor were to go in the ship that night he would die because of a huge storm - instead if he had been arrested, for a couple of days he would have been saved from a greater calamity.

The wallet should have gone to the poor man, because he would have used it in My service.

I was also going to reduce the rich man's karma by doing this, as well as save the sailor. But you canceled everything because of your attachment to do justice."

Krishna has plans and justice for everyone.... We just have to be patient!!!!!

RISING OUT OF THE DEEPEST WELL

One day a farmer's donkey fell down into a well. The animal cried piteously for hours as the farmer tried to figure out what to do. Finally, he decided that the animal was old, and the well needed to be covered up anyway; it just wasn't worth it to retrieve the donkey.

He invited all his neighbors to come over and help him. They all grabbed a shovel and began to shovel dirt into the well. At first, the donkey realized what was happening and cried horribly. Then, to everyone's amazement he quieted down. A few shovel loads later, the farmer finally looked down the well. He was astonished at what he saw. With each shovel of dirt that hit his back, the donkey was doing something amazing. He would shake it off and take a step up. As the farmer's neighbors continued to shovel dirt on top of the animal, he would shake it off and take a step up. Pretty soon, everyone was amazed as the donkey stepped up over the edge of the well and happily trotted off! In every step of life there are troubles. Life is going to shovel an amazing amount of dirt on you, all kinds of difficulties and troubles.

However, each of our troubles is a steppingstone to success. The trick is to get out of the well by shaking off what appears to be the end and take a step up.

Cinnamon Squares

You will need:
A deep 27x21cm
baking tray

Ingredients:
350g margarine
400g caster sugar
1 cup soya milk
350g plain flour
2 tsp baking powder
200g chopped dark
chocolate
150g light muscovado
sugar
2tsp cinnamon powder
100g cashew nuts

Method:

Mix muscovado sugar with cinnamon, set
aside. Mix first 5 ingredients and pour
into baking tray. Spread chocolate on the
top, then evenly spread the cinnamon
sugar and then the cashews. With your
palm gently press the surface. Bake for
40 min at 170c. When cool cut into
squares.

Coconut Cupcakes

You will need:

a muffin tin and
 paper cases

Ingredients:

40g dessicated coconut
175g icing sugar
200g plain flour
3 tbsp ground almonds
115g melted margarine
5 tbsp soya milk
For topping:
150g margarine
250g icing sugar
1 tsp vanilla essence

Method:

Mix all ingredients, spoon them into the
cases and bake them for 20 min or until a
fork comes out clean. Let them cool. Mix all
ingredients for the topping and top each
cupcake. Sprinkle coconut on them and
decorate with a cherry.

Coconut Slice

You will need:

A deep 27x21cm
baking tray

Ingredients:

150g margarine
300g self-raising flour
75g caster sugar
3 tbsp soya milk
1 tsp turmeric
1 jar raspberry jam
225g coconut
150g caster sugar
5 tbsp soya milk

Method:

Mix first five ingredients. Knead into a hard
dough. Press it into the bottom of tray to
cover the whole surface. Bake for 15 min on
170c. When ready spread jam over it. If the
Jam is too solid you can stir it in a bowl
before use. Mix remaining ingredients and
spread evenly on the jam. Press it down
lightly with your palm and bake it until the
surface gets golden.

Toffee Apple Cake

You will need:
A deep 27x21cm
baking tray

Ingredients:
375g apples peeled and diced
75g margarine
75g sugar
300g margarine
300g brown sugar
3/4 cup soya milk
300g self-raisig flour
1 tsp baking powder

Method:

Over medium heat melt the first margarine and sugar. Bring it to boil and let the sugar caramelise a bit. Add apples and cook till soft. Without the juice spread the apples evenly in the bottom of the tray. Mix remaining ingredients in a bowl and spoon over the apples. Bake for 45 min at 170c. While still hot pour the juice over the top. when cool cut into squares and serve it upside down.

Courgette Muffins

You will need:
a muffin tin and
 paper cases

Ingredients:
250g courgettes, grated
100g sultanas
4 tbsp orange juice
2 tbsp honey
6 tbsp soya milk
175ml sunflower oil
200g muscovado sugar
225g self-raising flour
1/2 tsp baking powder
1/2 tsp bicarbonate of soda
zest of 1 lemon

For topping
1 cup sunflower oil
3/4 cup soya milk
3/4 cup icing sugar
lemon juice

Method:
Boil sultanas, orange juice and honey in a pan
for 4 min. Whisk soya milk, oil and sugar in a
bowl. Squeeze liquid out from courgettes add
to the mix along with all other ingredients. Mix
well. spoon into cases and bake for 30 min on
180c. Blend topping ingredients while gradually
adding lemon juice until it becomes thick.
Spread on the top of cooled muffins.

HEAVEN AND HELL

Once upon a time, a man who had learned about the existence of heaven and hell was eager to know what these two places are, what the difference is between them.

He sincerely prayed to God, asking him to reveal the truth about the two realms. One night he received a revelation.

In his dream he met God, who said to him: "I understand that you want to see heaven and hell. I will take you to both places so you can see with your own eyes. First we will go to hell."

Then the scene changed. The man was looking upon a nice garden with flowers and freshly cut grass. Some people were sitting around on the grass. They all looked distraught and were suffering. As he looked closer he found that the arms of each person were tied to long wooden spoons. They could not put the food in the spoons into their mouths because the spoons were so long and as they bent their arms to feed, the spoons went past their face. In front of them there were plates of food but they were unable to eat.

"Now I'll take you to heaven," said the Lord.

The next scene was very much the same. The garden, the lawn and people sitting around. He even noticed the long wooden spoons tied to their arms, and the food in front of them. But to his amazement they looked happy and jolly.

Then he noticed that they were playfully feeding each other and were having fun.

"Do you understand now? The difference between heaven and hell is that in hell everyone is in it for themselves, while in heaven everyone is working together in cooperation and they are serving each other," concluded the merciful Lord.

THE KING'S QUESTION

Once upon a time there was a king in Gujarat, who was a very strict ruler, well known for his angry nature. One day he called all his ministers and said, "There has been a question in my mind for a long time and I cannot find the answer. It is now bothering me day and night. I want you to tell me the answer. The question is: 'Why does God come down to this Earth?'" He then dismissed his ministers and asked them to come back with the answer within a few days.

The ministers went to their apartment, packed their belongings and left the palace at once. As they walked, they came upon a peasant. The peasant was surprised to see all these nobles desperately trying to get away from the capitol. He stopped them to inquire about the reason.

"The king asked a question of us which we cannot answer. Therefore we flee for our lives because he will kill us if we admit our failure," said the nobles.

"So, what is that difficult question?" asked the peasant.

The nobles replied, "Why does God come down to this Earth?"

"Oh, I can answer that question."

"Really? Come with us then. We will take you to the King"

"Very well. Let's go!" said the peasant.

The ministers presented the peasant to the king.

"So, you know the answer to my question?" asked the King.

"Yes my lord."

"Let's hear it then."

"My lord, if I am to give you knowledge, then I should be seated higher than you."

"All right," said the king and stood up from his throne, sitting on a lower seat, as the peasant sat on the throne.

"God comes down to this earth to elevate the humble and humiliate the proud," came the answer.

MAYBE (Taoist story)

There is a Taoist story of an old farmer who had worked his crops for many years. One day his horse ran away. Upon hearing the news, his neighbours came to visit. "Such bad luck," they said sympathetically.

"Maybe," the farmer replied.

The next morning the horse returned, bringing with it three other wild horses. "How wonderful," the neighbors exclaimed.

"Maybe," replied the old man.

The following day, his son tried to ride one of the untamed horses, was thrown, and broke his leg. The neighbors again came to offer their sympathy on his misfortune.

"Maybe," answered the farmer.

The day after, military officials came to the village to draft young men into the army. Seeing that the son's leg was broken, they passed him by. The neighbors congratulated the farmer on how well things had turned out.

"Maybe," said the farmer.

Ginger Cake

You will need:

A deep 27x21cm
baking tray

Ingredients:

400ml soya milk
170g each dark
 muscovado sugar,
black treacle and golden syrup
130g finely grated ginger
170g melted margarine
1 1/2 tsp cinnamon
1 1/2 tsp mixed spice
1 1/2 tbsp ground ginger
350g self-raising flour
1/2 tsp bicarbonate of soda

Method:

Warm soya milk over a low heat with all the
sweet ingredients until they all melt. Pour into
a large bowl. Add all other ingredients. Mix
well, bake for 45 min on 170c. When cool
decorate with lemon icing. 2 tbsp lemon juice
mixed with icing sugar until you get the
consistency of single cream.

Lemon Drizzle Cake

You will need:
A deep 27x21cm baking tray

Ingredients:
150g margarine
260g golden caster sugar
1 cup soya milk
zest of 1 large lemon
260g self-raising flour
1 tsp baking powder
for the drizzle:
150g golden caster sugar
juice of 1 large lemon

Method:

Mix all cake ingredients using electric whisk until smooth. Bake it for 30 min or until an inserted fork comes out clean. Mix together the lemon juice and sugar, pour evenly over the cake while still hot, leave to cool.

Long Cake

You will need:
Approx 10x40 cm bread tin

Ingredients:

For cake:
Same as marble cake, but double amount (p 72)

For filling and topping:
200g margarine
400g icing sugar
1 tsp strawberry essence
1 tsp pink food colouring
400g chocolate melted

Method:
Mix all ingredients for a marble cake without the cocoa powder. Pour into the tin and bake for 30 min. When ready turn it onto a cooling rack. Mix all ingredients for a marble cake again with double cocoa powder. Bake it. When cakes are cool slice them 1 cm wide. Mix ingredients for the filling. Now assemble the cake: one white slice followed by a brown one and the pink icing in between each slice. When ready pour and spread chocolate over it. Cool it in the fridge. When serving cut the first slice diagonally and continue slicing parallel to it 1 1/2 cm each slices.

Fruity Cake

You will need:
2x22cm spring
form cake tin

Ingredients:
225 margarine
1/2 cup mango pulp
2 bananas
1 tsp vanilla extract
1/4 cup soya milk
140g muscovado sugar
50g fine dessicated
coconut
1/2 tsp cinnamon
powder
225g self-raising flour

For the topping:
600g tofu
2 cups icing sugar
4 tbsp mango pulp
4 tbsp coconut oil

Method:
Add all ingredients apart from flour into a
blender. Blend them until smooth. Then pour
mixture into a bowl and stir in the flour. Divide
between the two tins and bake for 30-35 min. To
make the topping first press the water out from
tofu. Put all ingredients into the blender. Blend
until smooth. Spread half on the top of one of
the cakes, then place the other cake on the top
and spread the rest of the topping on it.

KING MATTHEW THE JUST

King Matthew (1443 – 1490) was the most popular king of Hungary, famous for his justice.

One day a poor farmer was walking through the king's forest to reach the capitol, to sell his goods and pay his tax. As he was walking, he felt his back was itching terribly. To find some relief he leaned against a tree and started scratching his back. This didn't go unnoticed. A guard caught him and arrested him. A few days later he was presented in front of the king and accused of ruining the king's trees. When the king heard the details of the situation he decided that the farmer committed no crime and ordered twenty-five gold coins to be given to him, as compensation for the inconvenience caused to him.

The farmer felt much pride to have such righteous king. He happily arrived back to his village.

Of course the news of his good fortune spread quickly. In his village there lived two rich farmers who envied the fortune of the poor farmer. They agreed to do the same as the poor man did. Next day they were on their way to Buda through the king's forest. Half way there, they started to scratch their backs, leaning against a tree. They scratched until the guard came and arrested them.

Sure enough, in a few days' time they were standing in front of the king, who listened to their story. He then made his decision:

Twenty-five beatings with a stick on their backs.

The two men were shocked and protested: "But, my Lord, you have given twenty-five gold coins to the poor man from our village! Why are you punishing us for doing the same?!"

"He was on his own," came the answer, "- he couldn't scratch his own back. You could have scratched each others' back. You deserve punishment for your greed and envy."

THE JOYOUS DIVORCE

A woman was married for many years to her husband, but had not had children. Her husband decided to divorce her, so he went to Rabbi Shimon bar Yochai, of blessed memory.

Rabbi Shimon told him that just as they had celebrated with joy their mutual bond when they got married, so should the severance of their mutual bond be celebrated in joy.

The husband therefore prepared a great feast, at the height of which he called his wife and asked her in his joy to choose whatever she desired of his possessions to be hers, and said that he would not refuse her anything.

What did she do? She served him so much wine that he got drunk and fell asleep on his bed. She then told her servant to take him on his bed into her bedroom in her father's house.

The following morning, when he awoke and found himself in his wife's home, he asked her why he was brought there — wasn't it clear that he intended to divorce her? She replied, "Didn't you tell me that I could take whatever I wanted? I desire not gold, nor silver, nor precious gems, nor pearls. All I want is you. You yourself are the sole object of my desire."

When the husband heard this, he became once again enamored of his wife, and took her back as before. And in this merit the Holy One, blessed be He, granted them children.

Marble Cake

You will need:
22cm spring form cake tin

Ingredients:
225g margarine
225g caster sugar
3/4 cup soya milk
1 tsp vanilla extract
225g self-raising flour
2 tbsp cocoa powder

Method:
Mix all ingredients apart from the cocoa powder. Divide the mix into two and add cocoa powder to one. Mix well. Spoon into the baking tin taking turns between the two mixtures. Before you put it into the oven gently stir for a marble effect. Bake at 170c for 30 min or until a fork comes out clean. It is very nice on its own but you can also make a topping similar to the orange and chocolate cake topping. (p 52)

Pear Cake

You will need:
22cm spring form
cake tin greased

Ingredients:

200g margarine
150g light brown sugar
250g self-raising flour
1 tsp baking powder
1 tsp ground ginger
1 tsp cinnamon
1 orange zest and juice
8 tbsp soya milk
2 large pears peeled
and sliced

Method:
mix all ingredients apart from the pears.
Spread half the mixture in the cake tin.
Then spread the pear slices evenly and
cover them with the remaining mixture.
Optionally you can sprinkle demerara
sugar and flaked almonds on the top.
Bake for 45 min at 170c.

THE WISE DOG (Africa)

One day nine dogs went out to hunt. They met a lion.

He said, "I am hunting too. I am very, very hungry. Let us hunt together."

So the dogs and the lion hunted together all day. They caught ten antelopes.

Then the lion said, "Now we must divide this meat."

One of the dogs said, "Now, that's easy. We are ten, and we have ten antelopes. So, each of us will have one antelope."

The lion became very angry. He hit the poor dog and blinded him. The other dogs did not say a word. But then one of the dogs said, "Our brother was wrong. We must give nine antelopes to King Lion. Then they will be ten together. And we dogs shall take one antelope and we shall also be ten together."

The lion liked his answer and asked the dog, "Who taught you to divide like this? You are a wise dog."

The dog answered, "Oh, King Lion, you hit our brother and blinded him. That blind brother taught me, King Lion!"

Pumpkin Muffins

You will need:
a muffin tin and
 paper cases

Ingredients:

125g pumpkin or
butternut squash
grated
150ml sunflower oil
200ml soya milk
225g caster sugar
2 tsp ground ginger
75g walnut chopped
225g self-raising flour
1 tsp bicarbonate of
soda

Topping is the same as
courgette muffin with an
additional 1/2 tsp
cinnamon (p 62)

Method:
Add ingredients into a bowl and mix well.
Spoon into the cases and bake for 20-25
min at 180c. When cooled spread cinnamon
topping over the tops.

THE BLIND OLD LADY AND THE DOCTOR

An old lady suddenly became blind. Though she had spent a lot of money on medicine she could not get cured.

At last there came a doctor called Danbad, who said he would cure her if she gave him a large sum of money. She said she would give him the money when she was cured.

So the doctor came every day to treat her.

But he was a thief. Every day he took away something or other of the belongings of the old lady, first the boxes, then the chairs, then even the tables.

But he gave the lady good medicine and she was cured.

"Now," said the doctor, "give me my money."

"I won't," said the lady.

So the doctor took her to court.

But the lady told the judge: "I told the doctor I would pay him when I could see well. But I cannot see well. Before I was blind I could see tables and chairs and boxes in my house. Now I can see only bare walls. So I am not completely cured."

The judge understood and smiled. "Dr Danbad," he said, "unless you can make the lady see all her furniture and things, she shall not pay you."

That night the doctor went and quietly put back all the things he had taken from the lady's house.

THE POWER OF FAITH

In the medieval ages there were several crusades with the mission to go to Jerusalem, and bring the city under Christian rule. Of course there was a lot of opposition from the ruling Muslim armies.

Once, a crusade army set out on such expedition from France. They were outnumbered, struck by hunger and thirst. In spite of their determination they were defeated. Those who stayed alive camped for the night in the desert.

Next morning, one of the knights said to the others, "I had a wonderful dream. In my dream an angel came and said, 'Give up this despair. I bring you good news. Near your camp, buried under the sand, there is an old spear. This spear has pierced Lord Jesus's body before He was taken off the cross. Find this spear and go and fight again. Victory will be yours.' Then the angel disappeared and I suddenly woke up from my sleep. My tent had a heavenly scent. In my heart I know that it was more than just a dream. I suggest starting digging to find the spear."

The soldiers with great enthusiasm set out to dig up the desert. Sure enough the man who had the dream found the spear. Now with faith in the angel's words, they marched back to Jerusalem and fought again. Even though they were so few they came out victorious.

Many years later, when this man was on his deathbed he confessed. The spear belonged to his grandfather. Before he left home to go on the crusade, his grandmother asked him to take it with him. He wondered what he was going to do with an old, decrepit spear, but not wanting to disappoint his grandmother, he took it and carried it all the way.

Faith even if it is blind can empower one to do what is impossible.

Savories

Cheesy sticks

You will need:
flat baking tray lined
with greaseproof paper

Ingredients:
150g plain flour
150g cheese finely
grated
150g salted butter
1 tbsp sesami seeds

Method:
knead all ingredients together apart
from the sesami seeds. Add a little
water to get a medium soft dough. Roll
it out 5-6mm thick. Sprinkle with the
sesami seeds and press down slightly.
Cut into long rectangular shapes and
bake them for 15-20 min at 170c.

Greek Pie

You will need:
A deep 27x21cm baking tray

Ingredients:
1 ready rolled puffed pastry
2 tbsp olive oil
1/2 tsp hing
3x500g pack of spinach
250g chedar cheese
600g paneer or ricotta cheese
1 tbsp oregano
300 ml double cream
1 1/2 tsp salt
1/2 tsp black pepper

Method:
Press pastry into the baking tray and bake it for 10 min on 180c. Piercing the dough will prevent excessive puffing. Heat oil in a large sauce pan. Add hing and soon after the spinach with a small amount water to save it burning. Steam it a few min. When the pastry is ready spread some olive oil on it then spread spinach evenly. Sprinkle it with half the cheese, then spread the paneer or ricotta evenly on top. Sprinkle it with the rest of the cheese and oregano. Mix salt and pepper into the cream and pour over the pie. Bake it for 20 min at 180c.

Lasagne

You will need:
A deep 27x21cm baking tray

Ingredients:
For the white sauce:
100g butter
1 tsp hing
4 tbsp plain flour
1 l milk
1 tsp black pepper
1 tsp salt
200g chopped frozen spinach
a handful grated cheese

For the red sauce:
little olive oil
1 tsp hing
2 bay leaves
2 large carrots grated
5 piece of celery chopped
3 tins of chopped tomatoes
2 tsp brown sugar
1 box of lasgane pasta
Grated cheese

Method:
Make white sauce. Fry hing and flour in the butter and add milk. When thick add other ingredients. Make red sauce. Fry hing and bay leaves in oil add all other ingredients and cook until celery becomes soft. Cover the bottom of the tray with pasta then spread half of the red sauce. then a layer of pasta, then half of the white sauce and repeat again. finish with white sauce. Sprinkle with cheese and bake at 180c for 20 min.

Pasta Bake

You will need:
A deep 27x21cm
baking tray

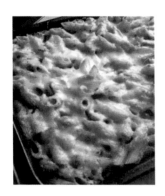

Ingredients:
300g pasta
1 tin chopped tomatoes
300 ml cream
2 tsp basil
olives
2 tsp salt
1 tsp pepper
1 tsp hing
grated cheese

Method:
Heat a couple of tablespoon of oil in a
saucepan. Add hing and fry for a few seconds.
Put all ingredients in a mixing bowl, but only a
handful of the cheese. Add boiling water until
it covers the pasta. Mix well. Spread it in the
baking tray and cover it with tin foil. Bake for
25-30 min at 180c. Remove the cover and
spread the cheese on top. Bake for another 10
min.

WRITE IN SAND, CARVE IN STONE

Two friends were walking through a desert. During some point in the journey, they had an argument and one of them slapped the other in the face. Although it hurt, he didn't say anything, but rather wrote in the sand: "Today my best friend slapped me in the face".

They kept on walking until they found an oasis where they decided to take a bath. The same one who got slapped got stuck in the mire and started drowning, but the friend saved him. After recovering from nearly drowning, he wrote on a stone: "Today my best friend saved my life".

His friend then asked him, "After I hurt you, you wrote in the sand and now on a stone. Why?"

The other replied, "When someone hurts us we should write it down in sand, where the winds of forgiveness can erase it away. But, when someone does something good for us, we must engrave it in stone where no wind can ever erase it. That is to say, learn to write your hurts in the sand and to carve your benefits in stone."

QUESTIONS

Maharaj Yudhisthira, by the power of his own virtues, became the emperor of the World. He was so pious that even his enemies respected him. Yet he was cheated out of his kingdom and sent into exile along with his four brothers, who were the greatest warriors of the time.

During their time in the forest they all became fatigued and thirsty. The youngest of the brothers climbed on a tall tree to see if there was any water nearby.

He noticed a lake a short distance away. He left to fetch some water for all of them.

As he tried to get the water from the lake, he heard a deep voice:

"This lake is mine. You cannot take the water unless you answer my questions. If you try you will die."

He looked around, looking for the source of the voice, but he only saw a crane in the water. Ignoring the voice he proceeded to drink some water and fill up his pot. Suddenly he fell dead on the shore.

One by one Yudhisthira's brothers came to the lake, but the same thing happened to them.

Yudhisthira became more and more anxious as none of his brothers returned. He then approached the lake and found all his powerful brothers dead. His eyes were full of tears as he called their names, but no answer. He noticed that their bodies, even though lifeless, didn't lose their luster. There was no sign of fight and no blood anywhere. He was bewildered. "Maybe the water is poisoned," he thought to himself.

As he got close to the lake he heard the deep voice: "This lake is mine. You cannot take the water unless you answer my questions. If you try you will die."

Surprised, he looked around to see who was talking, but only saw the crane in the water. "Please ask your questions and if I can I will try to answer them," said King Yudhisthira respectfully.

The crane then asked deep philosophical and moral questions and Yudhisthira answered them all.

Finally the crane said, "Here is my last and most difficult question: What is the most wonderful thing in the world?"

Yudhisthira stopped to think for a moment and said: "The most wonderful thing in the world is that everyone experiences that all living entities are doomed to die, yet everyone is living as if they will live forever."

The voice said: "I am very pleased with you. Know me as Yamaraj, the God of Death. You can have your brothers back and I am sure that one day you will be emperor again. Then righteousness will once again prevail."

Pasties

You will need:
flat baking tray lined
with greaseproof paper

Ingredients:
For filling:
1 large potato boiled
and mashed
200g cottage cheese
200g frozen mixed veg
1 1/2 tsp salt
1 tsp black pepper
2 tsp rosemary
grated cheese for the
top

For pastry:
300g plain flour
3/4 tsp salt
1 tsp paprika
1 tbsp tomato puree
100g butter
5-6 tbsp water.

Method:
Mix all ingredients for the pastry and knead for
a few min. You need a hardish dough. Mix all
ingredients for the filling. Divide the dough into
six parts and roll the first one out into a 5mm
thick circle. Place a serving of the filling in the
middle and pick up two opposite sides and
press them together and fold up the corners.
Place on the baking tray then flatten gently.
When all are done spread cheese on top and
bake for 25-30 min at 180c.

Spinach Muffins

You will need:
a muffin baking tray

Ingredients:

25g butter, plus extra for
greasing
200ml milk
100g frozen chopped
spinach squeezed
250g plain flour
1 tbsp baking powder
1 tsp bicarbonate soda
1/2 tsp cayenne pepper
2 tbsp yoghurt
200g soft cheese
50g cheddar grated

Method:
Melt the butter in the milk over low heat, than add
spinach. Mix in next 6 ingredients.
Mix well, th n put half of the mixture into 10 of the
muffin holes then put a heaped tablespoon of the
soft cheese then the rest of the mixture. Sprinkle
them with the cheddar and bake them for 25 min
at 180c. Leave to cool in the tray for 5 min then
turn out onto a wire rack.

Potato Bake

You will need:
A deep 27x21cm
baking tray

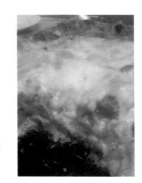

Ingredients:
600 ml single cream
1 tsp hing
2 tsp salt
1 tsp black pepper
4 potatoes thinly sliced
1 tblsp rosemary
grated cheese

Method:

Place potatoes into baking tray forming
layers. Mix first four ingredients and pour
over the potatoes. Sprinkle with rosemary.
Bake on 180c for 45 min. Then spread
cheese on top and bake for another 10-15
min until cheese browns.

Stuffed Courgettes

You will need:
35x25cm deep baking
tray greased

Ingredients:
4 medium courgettes
2 tbsp oil
1 tsp hing
1 tin sweetcorn (300g)
200g soft cheese
salt, pepper
2 tsp rosemary
200g grated cheddar

Method:

Cook courgettes until tender. Drain and cut off
the stem. Cut them half in longwise and scoop
out the middle. Place them on the baking tray
with their middle facing up.
Heat oil, add hing and a few seconds later the
sweetcorn. Optionally you can add a little
tomato puree at this point. Add a little water
and the the middle of the courgettes you
scooped out and boil it for a few min. Then
remove from the heat and add cheese, salt,
pepper and herbs. Mix well. Spoon this mixture
into the courgettes and sprinkle with cheese.
Bake them for 15-20 min at 180c.

TAKING RESPONSIBILITY TO MOVE FORWARD

Once there was a man who liked to eat mangoes. One day he decided to get the sweetest mango available, from the very top of the tree. Mangoes which are most exposed to the sun are the sweetest. So he climbed up to the top, where the branches were thin. He managed to pick up a few sweet reddish fruits, but in attempting to go back down, he slipped and started falling towards the ground.

Fortunately, he caught a branch as he was falling and remained helplessly hanging on the tree. Then he started to call nearby villagers for help. They immediately came with a ladder and sticks, but could do little to help him.

Then after some time, one calm and thoughtful person arrived - a well-known sage who lived in a simple hut nearby. People were very curious as to what he would do, since he was very famous for solving many people's problems in the area, sometimes very complicated ones. He was silent for a minute and then picked up a stone, and threw it, hitting the man.

Everybody was surprised.

Hanging mango lover started to shout, "What are you doing?! Are you crazy? Do you want me to break my neck?"

The sage was silent. Then again, he took a stone and threw it, so that it hit the man in the tree.

The man was furious, "If I could just come down, I would show you...!" That's what everybody wanted, that he comes down, but how?Now everybody was tense, what would happen next? Some wanted to chastise the sage, but they didn't. The sage picked up another stone and threw it again at the man, even more forcefully. Now the man in the tree completely flipped out and developed a great determination to come down and get revenge.

He then used all of his skill and strength and somehow managed to reach the branches which were safe enough for him to climb down, and he made it!

Everybody was amazed.

"Where is the sage?!" exclaimed the rescued man.

"Oh, he is a wise man, so he didn't wait for you to beat him," said the villagers.

"I will really smash him completely when I get hold of him," said the man.

"Hey, wait a minute, he is the only one who helped you, he is the one who provoked you, who induced you to help yourself," said one of the villagers.

Mango freak stopped for a second, thought a little and admitted, "Yes, all your good intentions and compassion didn't help me, but the sage expertly induced me to do my best and save myself. I should be thankful rather than angry."

So this is an instructive leadership story. A real leader (teacher) helps you, sometimes in strange ways, to take initiatives in your life. You have to move forward. You have to make your best effort if you want extraordinary results. The best leader helps you to be responsible for your life.

DON'T HURT YOURSELF

While touring the country to impart his teachings to people, a spiritual teacher reached a village in which the headman disliked holy men. He was very much irritated when anybody talked about Krishna.

When this village headman came to know that the guru was coming to their village along with his disciples that day for begging alms, he called a meeting of all the villagers and ordered them,

"Nobody should offer alms to this guru when he comes to our village to beg alms today; don't even open the doors of your houses when he comes." He himself also put a lock on the door of his house and sat on the porch in front of it.

When the holy man came to the house of the headman, he stood in front of it and called "Bhagavati Bhiksham Dehi (Mother, give alms)."

The village headman at once flew into a rage on hearing this. He said to him, "Oh lazy mendicant! You have no work to do except to fill your belly by begging. On top of it, you are ruining the lives of so many young men by making them your disciples. You have no right teaching others!" he shouted. "You are as stupid as everyone else. You are nothing but a fake. Go away from here and earn your living by hard work."

Without even a bit of agitation, the holy man said smilingly to the headman, "Sir, I have a query. Will you kindly resolve it?"

"What is the query?" thundered the headman. Then the teacher said, "Tell me, if you buy a gift for someone, and that person does not take it, to whom does the gift belong?"

The man was surprised to be asked such a strange question and answered, "It would belong to me, because I bought the gift."

The holy man then smiled and said, "You have given the correct reply. I came to your house and begged for alms. But you gave me the alms of abuse, which I decline to accept. To whom will these abuses then return? You yourself gave the answer.

"If you become angry with me and I do not get insulted, then the anger falls back on you. You are then the only one who becomes unhappy, not me. All you have done is hurt yourself.

"If you want to stop hurting yourself, you must get rid of your anger and become loving instead. When you hate others, you yourself become unhappy. But when you love others, everyone is happy."

The village headman did not know what to say. He fell at the feet of the guru and prayed for his forgiveness.

ABOUT ATMA LOUNGE

Aberystwyth is a beautiful small town and a popular holiday destination   in Wales, United Kingdom. It also has a University and a lot of art and cultural interest. The town is surrounded with stunning countryside with a very positive vibe. This whole situation attracts spiritually minded people. The locals are very friendly and accommodating.

We opened the Atma Lounge here to give an opportunity for anyone interested to learn about and experience the culture and wisdom of the Vedas from ancient India.

We offer yoga and meditation classes, and are planning for more courses such as Ayurveda (health and self-healing).

You can come here to relax and rejuvenate mentally and spiritually with sound therapy, musical meditation, counselling and massage.

You can have a bit of fun with traditional henna mehandi designs on your hand.

You can shop for gifts, clothes, books ethically sourced from India and Nepal. In our shop we have also created an outlet for devotee artworks.

Our guests learn about the philosophy and spiritual practices of the Bhagavad-Gita and have an amazing vegetarian feast every Sunday.

(sees details on www.facebook.com/atmalounge or www.atmalounge.com)
We invite you and your friends and family to come and take part in any of these programmes. We can organize accommodation if needed.

We also have more plans for the future
We would like to open more centres like this in other places in Wales.

We also planning to create a retreat centre where we can introduce more aspects of the Vedic culture. With the motto of "simple living, high thinking". Here you will be able to gain a deeper experience about living with spiritual values.

We are very passionate about creating a friendly and welcoming atmosphere for everyone. We are spiritual practitioners in ISKCON for over 20 years. We are trying to follow the loving and encouraging mood of A.C. Bhaktivedanta Swami Srila Prabhupada the Founder-Acarya of the International Society of Krishna Consciousness and his dear disciple HH Kesava Bharati Dasa Goswami.

If you like what we are doing you can show your appreciation by donating on our website:
www.atmalounge.com

Thank you very much
Your servants
Priya Kunda das
Syama Gauri devi dasi

Printed in Great Britain
by Amazon